The
World's Best
Dirty Songs

Don Laycock

The World's Best Dirty Songs

Illustrations by Louis Silvestro

ANGUS
& ROBERTSON
PUBLISHERS

ANGUS & ROBERTSON PUBLISHERS

Unit 4, Eden Park, 31 Waterloo Road,
North Ryde, NSW, Australia 2113, and
16 Golden Square, London W1R 4BN,
United Kingdom

First published in Australia by
Angus & Robertson Publishers in 1986
First published in the United Kingdom by
Angus & Robertson (UK) Ltd in 1986
Reprinted 1987, 1988

Copyright © Donald C. Laycock 1986

ISBN 0 207 15408 2

Typeset in 12pt Palatino by
New Faces, Bedford
Printed in the United Kingdom by
Hazell Watson & Viney Limited

INTRODUCTION

The men of Great Britain, Australia, America, Canada – in fact, of all the countries of the world to which the English language has been transported – share one thing in common: their love for the dirty song, whether it be rendered in the clubhouse after a football game, in an army camp, around the keg at a party, or in the remote communal huts of a struggling farm.

Speakers of other languages don't have the same feeling for this art form. The French are so insensitive that they sing their dirty songs in public, and in mixed company, in the bistros, and in the street. The Germans are a bit more reserved, and confine their bawdry to bucolic harvest festivals and the forced joviality of beerfests. If the song mentions the backside it is a big hit. The Italians, who have a wide erotic vocabulary when they put their minds to it, would just as soon sing romantic songs about returning to Napoli. The Russians deny that they have any dirty songs in their language at all; certainly no one would dream of singing them in a country that has banned the printing of all obscene words, even in dictionaries, for over two hundred years.

Only in an English-speaking country does the dirty song flourish in its pristine purity, as an activity of males denied – or terrified of – any other outlet for their sexuality. The dirty song is a collective male fantasy, of what the singer would like to do with a woman, or women, if only . . . That being so, it is understandable that many women do not like the sentiments expressed in dirty songs, though they can enjoy them for the simplicity of their emotions and the folk naivety of their expression.

Dirty songs simply do not survive unless they are first-rate examples of popular wit, though a rousing melody helps, of course. Presented here in cold print, the songs do not have the power that they have when bellowed out melodically by a group of thirty drunken males (though, admittedly, they are much safer and nicer to be near). For this reason, an indication of the melodies has been provided wherever possible.

Ideally, of course, the songs should be passed on by word of mouth, and not set down in stark and sterile print. But in an age where little is passed on orally but herpes, this little book of the best, and best-known, dirty songs in the English language ensures that you can enjoy your heritage in the privacy and comfort of your own living-room.

And then go down to the pub or club to sing them.

Don Laycock

ABDUL ABULBUL EMIR

To its own traditional tune.

O the harems of Egypt are fair to behold
and the maidens are fairer than fair
and two hundred a week weren't enough for the
    Sheikh
named Abdul Abulbul Emir.

A travelling brothel was brought to the town
by a Russian who came from afar;
he wagered a buck no one could outshuck
Count Ivan Skavinsky Skavar.

The peasants did shout when the announcement
    came out
in an ad in the *Gulf Gazetteer*
and plunged into debt to get in their bet
on Abdul Abulbul Emir.

For Abdul would ride with his bride by his side,
his face all flushed with desire;
he had it decried that he could outride
Count Ivan Skavinsky Skavar.

It was only the Jews who wagered he'd lose
with the slander their prince was a queer;
but the rest of the Persians would believe no
    perversions
of Abdul Abulbul Emir.

Count Ivan agreed, Prince Abdul agreed,
to compete in the city's bazaar;
ten merchants were shot, to secure a clear spot
for Abdul and Ivan Skavar.

The crowd all got smashed on Kashmiri hash
washed down with Lebanese beer
for which the concession was held by a Circassian
kinsman of Abdul Emir.

A spectacle great was arranged for the date,
'twas agreed on by Sultan and Czar;
the streets were all lined with cheergirls entwined
round Abdul and Ivan Skavar.

The Sultan rode by with a wide open fly
expecting the women to cheer,
but all eyes were fixed on the two massive pricks
of Ivan and Abdul Emir.

Czar Petrovitch II attended the do,
with a telescope watched from afar,
while one of his band pulled him off in the sand
as a tribute to Ivan Skavar.

They stood on the track with their tools hanging
    slack,
the starter's gun punctured the air;
both quick on the rise, all gasped at the size
of Abdul Abulbul Emir.

The harlots were shorn, no frenchies were worn;
Abdul's arse revved up like a car;

but he couldn't compete with the long even beat
of Ivan Skavinsky Skavar.

Now Ivan had won and was cleaning his gun
and bent down to polish his pair
when he felt something hot pass right up his blot –
'twas Abdul Abulbul Emir.

The harlots turned green and the men shouted
    'Queen!'
– they were ordered apart by the Czar –
but alas they were stuck; it was jolly bad luck
for Ivan Skavinsky Skavar.

They needed a crane, a tractor and chain
to rescue the unfortunate peer;
Ivan said in a huff, 'I've had quite enough
of this Abdul Abulbul Emir.'

Now the cream of the joke, when at last they were
    broke,
was laughed at for years by the Shah;
for Abdul, the fool, had left half of his tool
in the arse of Skavinsky Skavar.

The moral, dear friend, of this pitiful end
is plain for all who hear:
when seeking your bit, don't get stuck in the shit
like Abdul Abulbul Emir.

THE BALL OF KIRRIEMUIR

To its own traditional tune.

O the ball, the ball, the ball, the ball, the ball at
    Kirriemuir,
there were four-and-twenty prostitutes a-lying on
    the floor

    singing, 'Who'll do me this time,
    who'll do me now?
    The one that did me last time
    cannot do me now.'

And when the ball had started, they all began to
    jig;
before a half an hour had passed, they all began
    to frig

First lady forward, second lady back,
third lady's finger up the fourth lady's crack.

Fifth lady forward, sixth lady pass,
seventh lady's finger up the eighth lady's arse.

There were four-and-twenty virgins came down
    from Inverness,
and when the ball was over there were four-and-
    twenty less

singing, 'Who'll do me this time,
who'll do me now?
The one that did me last time
had to show me how.'

The Elders of the Kirk were there, and very
surprised to see,
four-and-twenty maidenheads a-hanging on a tree.

There was rooting in the rafters, there was rooting
in the ricks,
and you couldn't hear the music for the swishing
of the pricks.

There was screwing in the bedrooms, there was
screwing in the halls,
and you couldn't hear the bagpipes for the
clanging of the balls.

There was screwing in the doorways, there was
screwing on the stairs,
and you couldn't see the carpet for the come and
curly hairs.

The minister, yes he was there, he wasna' feeling
weel,
he couldna' hold his water in the middle of the
reel.

The chimney-sweep, now he was there, they had
to chuck him oot,
for every time he broke his wind, he filled the
room with soot.

The village harlot, she was there, keeping the boys
    in fits,
by swinging from the chandeliers and landing on
    her tits.

The village blacksmith, he was there, a-sitting on
    the mat,
amusing himself by abusing himself, and catching
    it in his hat.

The village cripple, he was there, he wasn't up to
    much,
lining 'em up against the wall and stuffing 'em
    with his crutch.

The village idiot, he was there, up to his usual trick
of pulling his foreskin over his head, and whistling
    down his prick.

The village doctor, he was there, with his bag of
    tricks,
amusing himself between each dance by
    circumcising pricks.

The village postman, he was there, with addresses
    hard to find,
but the only letters that he had were of a foreign
    kind.

The postman's brother, he was there, and scared to
    death of pox;
he wouldn't stuff the sheilas so he stuffed the
    letter-box.

Jock the parson, he was there, it was a bloody
    shame;
loved a lassie thirty times and never knew her
    name.

The village barber, he was there, his razor in his
    hand,
and every time the music stopped he'd circumcise
    the band.

The undertaker, he was there, dressed in his long
    white shroud,
squatting on the chandelier and pissing on the
    crowd.

The motor mechanic, he was there, down before
    the fire,
having sexual intercourse with a punctured Dunlop
    tyre.

The old schoolmaster he was there, working out
    a sum;
he figured out by logarithms the time that he would
    come.

The local prankster, he was there, up to his usual
    farce,
of sticking his head between his legs and sliding
    up his arse.

The village plumber, he was there, he felt an awful
    fool;
he'd come eleven leagues or more and forgot to
    bring his tool.

The vicar and his wife were there, having lots of
    fun;
the vicar had his finger up another lady's bum.

The verger played a dirty trick, we cannot let it pass;
he showed a girl his mighty rod, then shoved it up
    her arse.

The village builder, he was there, with a barrow-
    load of bricks;
he poured cement in all the holes, and blunted all
    the pricks.

The butcher's boy, he was there, the leader of the
    choir;
he bashed the balls of all the boys to make their
    voices higher.

The village barber, he was there, and he was in
    despair;
he couldn't get his curling-iron through the tangles
    of the hair.

The papal delegate, he was there, he lectured to
    the room:
'The vagina, not the rectum, is the right way to the
    womb.'

Tarzan of the Apes was there, acting like a fool,
jumping from the rafters and swinging on his
    tool.

The village women, they were there, sitting in
    a ring,

knitting contraceptives from a batch of rubber
string.

The queen was in the parlour, eating bread and
honey,
the king was in the chambermaid, and she was in
the money.

Dr Livingstone he was there, striving hard to
please,
by giving lantern lectures on venereal disease.

Madam Blavatsky she was there, leading the free
life,
and all the men could testify she was a model wife.

Winston Churchill, he was there, down behind the
bar,
and when he couldn't get it up, he used his big
cigar.

The Bishop of Ely, he was there, to screw he would
not stoop,
he'd always been a bugger since he joined the
Oxford group.

Queen Victoria, she was there, trying to be nice,
and before the ball was over she'd only been laid
twice.

Among the many visitors was Dr Marie Stopes;
she made no fancy promises, but she raised a lot
of hopes.

Woody Guthrie, he was there, singing of the dust,
till he throwed his old guitar away and yielded up
to lust.

Oscar Wilde, he was there, bowed down with age
and caries,
digging round the toadstools and looking for the
fairies.

Joe McCarthy, he was there, looking in the beds,
but these were filled with heteros, and not with
pansy reds.

O, there was screwing in the farmyard, screwing in
the byre;
the friction of the arseholes set all the hay on fire.

O, the ball, the ball, the ball, the ball, the ball of
Kirriemuir,
some came for the dancing, but most came there to
whore.

And when the ball was over, we all went home to
rest;
we said the music wasn't bad, but the screwing
was the best.

MY SISTER ELIZABETH

To the tune of "The Ash Grove".

My sister Elizabeth
has gonorrhoea and syphilis

> *And the hairs on her dinky-di-do*
> *hang down to her knees.*
> *One red one, one white one,*
> *and one with a bit of shite on,*
> *the hairs on her dinky-di-do*
> *hang down to her knees.*

I've seen 'em, I've cleaned 'em,
I've actually been between 'em.

I've stroked 'em, I've poked 'em,
I've even rolled 'em up and smoked 'em.

It would take a Welsh miner
to find her vagina.

If she were my daughter
I'd have 'em cut shorter.

Though it may seem ridiculous
she rides her bike knickerless.

She lives on a mountain
and pisses like a bloody fountain.

She went to the varsity
and there lost her blasted chastity.

She went to Port Kembla
and there got a knee-trembler.

She went to Newcastle
and there got it up the arsehole.

She has a companion
with balls like a bloody stallion.

I've touched it, I've felt it,
it felt like a bit of velvet.

> *And the hairs on her dinky-di-do*
> *hang down to her knees.*
> *One black one, one blue one,*
> *and one with a little screw on,*
> *the hairs (and the hairs!)*
> *on her dinky-di-do (dinky-di-do!),*
> *and the hairs on her dinky-di-do*
> *hang down to her knees.*

MY GOD HOW THE MONEY ROLLS IN

To the tune of "My Bonnie Lies Over the Ocean".

I've shares in the very best companies,
in tramways, tobacco, and tin,
in brothels in Rio de Janeiro –
my God how the money rolls in.

> *Rolls in, rolls in,*
> *my God how the money rolls in, rolls in;*
> *rolls in, rolls in,*
> *my God how the money rolls in.*

With wealth in the big German steelworks,
no wonder I helped Hitler win,
for when he suppressed the trade unions,
my God how the money rolled in.

My father sent field guns to Franco,
my brother raised loans for Berlin,
my uncle sent scrap-iron to Tojo,
to make sure that the money rolled in.

My cousin's a starting-price bookie,
my mother makes synthetic gin,
my sister sells sin to the sailors –
my God how the money rolls in.

My mother's a bawdy-house keeper;
each night as the street lights grow dim
she hangs a red light in the window –
my God how the money rolls in.

My brother's a curate in Sydney,
he saves little girlies from sin;
he'll save you a blonde for a dollar –
my God how the money rolls in.

We've started an old-fashioned gin-shop,
a regular palace of sin;
the principal girl is my grandma –
my God how the money rolls in.

My grandmother's well over eighty,
but can still urinate in a tin;
we sell it as patented corn-cure –
my God how the money rolls in.

My sister's a barmaid in Bondi;
for a dollar she'll strip to the skin;
she's stripping from morning to midnight –
my God how the money rolls in.

My aunt keeps a girls' seminary,
teaching young girls to begin;
she doesn't say where they're to finish –
my God how the money rolls in.

My dad manufactures French letters,
my sister makes holes with a pin;

my uncle arranges abortions –
my God how the money rolls in.

My cousin's a Harley Street surgeon,
with instruments long, sharp and thin;
he only does one operation –
my God how the money rolls in.

Uncle Arthur's a registered plumber,
doing business in holes and in tin;
he'll plug up your hole for a dollar –
my God how the money rolls in.

My nephew is carving out candles
from wax that is surgically soft;
he hopes it will still keep him going
if ever his business falls off.

My brother's a poofter in Chelsea,
you can't hear him jerk for the din;
his mother makes lotion for sore bums –
my God how the money rolls in.

My daughter now preaches hot gospel,
she's forsworn the rest of her kin.
We know that she now can afford to,
my God how the money rolls in.

I've lost all my cash on the horses,
I'm sick from the illicit gin;
I'm falling in love with my father –
my God what a mess I am in.

IN MOBILE

To the tune of "She'll Be Coming Round the Mountain".

How I love to see that bosom pal o' mine,
how I love to see that bosom pal o' mine,
how I love to see that bosom,
how I love to see that bosom,
how I love to see that bosom pal o' mine.

Singing I will if you will, so will I,
Singing I will if you will, so will I,
Singing I will if you will,
I will if you will,
Singing I will if you will, so will I.

O she has a lovely pair of big blue eyes,
O she has a lovely pair of big blue eyes,
O she has a lovely pair,
she has a lovely pair,
she has a lovely pair of big blue eyes.

O she has a lovely bottom set of teeth,
O she has a lovely bottom set of teeth,
O she has a lovely bottom,
she has a lovely bottom,
she has a lovely bottom set of teeth.

O she has a lovely naval uniform,
O she has a lovely naval uniform,

O she has a lovely navel,
she has a lovely navel,
she has a lovely naval uniform.

O I'd like to take her pants down to the cleaners,
O I'd like to take her pants down to the cleaners,
O I'd like to take her pants down,
I'd like to take her pants down,
I'd like to take her pants down to the cleaners.

I'd like to give her a length of pretty lace,
I'd like to give her a length of pretty lace,
I'd like to give her a length,
I'd like to give her a length,
I'd like to give her a length of pretty lace.

O I gave my girl a baby Austin car,
O I gave my girl a baby Austin car,
O I gave my girl a baby,
I gave my girl a baby,
I gave my girl a baby Austin car.

O she loves to see a pianist perform,
O she loves to see a pianist perform,
O she loves to see a penis,
she loves to see a penis,
she loves to see a pianist perform.

O she has a lovely country residence,
O she has a lovely country residence,
and the flowers in the garden
are just like the Vale of Arden,
O she has a lovely country residence.

O the eagles they fly high in Mobile,
O the eagles they fly high in Mobile,
O the eagles they fly high,
and they shit right in your eye – ·
thank Christ the cows don't fly in Mobile.

In Mobile! In Mobile!
In Mo- in Mo- in Mo- in Mobile!
O the eagles they fly high
and they shit right in your eye –
thank Christ the cows don't fly in Mobile!

O the parson is perverted in Mobile,
O the parson is perverted in Mobile,
O the parson is perverted
and his morals are inverted
and there's thousands he's converted in Mobile.

O the bishop is a bugger in Mobile,
O the bishop is a bugger in Mobile,
O the bishop is a bugger
and his brother is another
and they bugger one another in Mobile.

There's a girl called Lady Dinah in Mobile,
there's a girl called Lady Dinah in Mobile,
there's a girl called Lady Dinah,
and you'll say once you grind her
that she's got the best vagina in Mobile.

There's a shortage of good whores in Mobile,
there's a shortage of good whores in Mobile,

there's a shortage of good whores,
but there's keyholes in the doors,
and knotholes in the floors in Mobile.

Frenchies are in short supply in Mobile,
frenchies are in short supply in Mobile,
frenchies are in short supply
and so that's the reason why
they hang them out to dry in Mobile.

There's no paper in the bogs in Mobile,
there's no paper in the bogs in Mobile,
there's no paper in the bogs,
they just wait until it clogs,
then they saw it off in logs in Mobile.

O they don't use boggus paper in Mobile,
O they don't use boggus paper in Mobile,
they don't use boggus paper,
they don't hold with no such caper,
they just use a putty scraper in Mobile.

Virgins are very rare in Mobile,
virgins are very rare in Mobile,
virgins are very rare
'cos when they get their pubic hair
they get rooted by the mayor in Mobile.

There's a virgin, so they say, in Mobile,
there's a virgin, so they say, in Mobile,
there's a virgin, so they say,
she was born just yesterday,
but the navy's on its way to Mobile.

O the girls all wear tin pants in Mobile,
O the girls all wear tin pants in Mobile,
O the girls all wear tin pants
but they take them off to dance –
everybody gets his chance in Mobile.

There's a lack of fornication in Mobile,
there's a lack of fornication in Mobile,
there's a lack of fornication
but there's lots of masturbation –
and that's the situation in Mobile.

O the students get no tail in Mobile,
O the students get no tail in Mobile,
O the students get no tail,
so they bang it on the rail –
it's the arsehole of creation, is Mobile.

There's a man called Dirty Keith in Mobile,
there's a man called Dirty Keith in Mobile,
there's a man called Dirty Keith
and he wears a laurel wreath
of pubic hairs around his teeth in Mobile.

There's a naughty boy called Danny in Mobile,
there's a naughty boy called Danny in Mobile,
there's a naughty boy called Danny
and he likes his bit of fanny
and he gets it off his granny in Mobile.

There's a stupid man called Green in Mobile,
there's a stupid man called Green in Mobile,
there's a stupid man called Green,

and he thinks he is a queen,
but he's got a ruptured spleen in Mobile.

O they have a pet aversion in Mobile,
O they have a pet aversion in Mobile,
the aversion was a virgin
but she didn't take much urgin';
soon the penises were surgin' in Mobile.

O the men they wash the dishes in Mobile,
O the men they wash the dishes in Mobile,
O the men they wash the dishes
and they dry them on their breeches –
O the dirty sons-of-bitches, in Mobile!

O the cows they all are dead in Mobile,
O the cows they all are dead in Mobile,
O the cows they all are dead
so they milk the bulls instead,
because babies must be fed in Mobile.

If you ever go to jail in Mobile,
if you ever go to jail in Mobile,
if you ever go to jail
and you need a piece of tail,
the sheriff's wife's for sale in Mobile.

Gentlemen of the working classes in Mobile,
gentlemen of the working classes in Mobile,
gentlemen of the working classes
when you've finished with your glasses
you can stuff 'em up your arses in Mobile.

When the tax collector calls in Mobile,
when the tax collector calls in Mobile,
when the tax collector calls
they cut off both his balls
and they nail them to the walls in Mobile.

O we won't go back to Subic from Mobile,
O we won't go back to Subic from Mobile,
O we won't go back to Subic –
the mosquitoes there are too big
and they bite you in the pubic in Mobile.

O the girls don't smell like roses in Mobile,
O the girls don't smell like roses in Mobile,
O the girls don't smell like roses
but they know a hundred poses
so you needn't hold your noses in Mobile.

THE GOOD SHIP VENUS

To the tune of "In and Out the Window".

It was on the good ship *Venus*,
by Christ you should have seen us;
the figurehead was a whore in bed
astride a rampant penis.

> *Frigging in the rigging,*
> *frigging in the rigging,*
> *we're frigging in the rigging*
> *'cos there's nothing else to do.*

It was at the China station,
by way of celebration,
we sunk a junk with jets of spunk
by mutual masturbation.

We sailed to the Canaries
to screw the local fairies;
we got the syph in Tenerife
and the clap in Buenos Aires.

We sailed to the Bahamas
where the girls all wear pyjamas;
they wouldn't screw our motley crew –
they much preferred bananas.

The captain's name was Mugger,
a dirty-minded bugger;

he wasn't fit to shovel shit
from one deck to the other.

The first mate's name was Morgan,
a homosexual Gorgon;
six men could ride with legs astride
upon his sexual organ.

The second mate's name was Abel;
his arsehole bore this label:
'I'll give the crew their daily due
though I'm no Betty Grable.'

The third mate's name was Walter;
at love he'd never falter.
The bloody stiff had given syph
to all the girls in Malta.

The stoker was McGuire,
he really was a trier,
for though on shore he kept a whore,
on board he pulled his wire.

The steward's name was Topper;
boy did he have a whopper!
Twice round the deck, once round his neck,
and up his arse for a stopper.

The bosun's name was Andy,
a bastard bald and bandy;
they filled his bum with boiling rum
for pissing in the brandy.

But the bosun's plan was prosperous:
he dipped his cock in phosphorus;
all through the night it kept alight
to guide us through the Bosporus.

The purser's name was Lester;
he was a hymen tester;
through hymens thick he'd shove his prick
and leave it there to fester.

That purser came from Wigan;
by God he had a big 'un!
We bashed his cock with a lump of rock
for frigging in the rigging.

The fireman was McTavish,
and young girls he did ravish;
his missing tool's in Istanbul –
he was a trifle lavish.

The carpenter Carruthers,
beloved of all the others;
he wasn't quite hermaphrodite,
but a mistake of his mother's.

The engineer McPherson
to snatch had an aversion
so he stuck his cock up a water-chock –
a peculiar perversion!

The musician's name was Carter;
he tuned his arse as a farter.
He could play anything from God Save the King
to Beethoven's Moonlight Sonata.

The cook's name was O'Malley,
he didn't dilly-dally;
he shot his bolt with such a jolt
he whitewashed half the galley.

The cook's offsider Riemann,
he was a filthy demon;
he served the crew a filthy brew
of foreskins boiled in semen.

A third cook's name was Aiken;
each morning he'd awaken
and scrape the spunk from off his bunk
to fry the skipper's bacon.

The trainee cook was Wooden,
by Christ he was a good 'un;
he tossed off twice in a bag of rice
and called it sago puddin'.

The radio operator
he was a masturbator;
to get a jolt he'd shoot his bolt
across the oscillator.

A stowaway named Tupper,
we rubbed his balls with butter;
the charge whizzed past the mizzen mast
and foamed against the scupper.

The stewardess was Dinah,
she sprang a leak off China;
we had to pump poor Dinah's rump
to empty her vagina.

The cabin-boy's name was Nipper,
a dirty little flipper;
they filled his arse with broken glass
and circumcised the skipper.

The ladies of the nation
arose in indignation
and stuffed his bum with chewing-gum –
a smart retaliation!

The captain's wife was Mabel,
always willing and able,
behind the door, or on the floor,
or on the chart room table.

The captain had a daughter,
she fell into the water;
ecstatic squeals revealed that eels
had found her sexual quarter.

When we put into Calais,
the captain's daughter, Sally,
dressed as a whore she rushed ashore
and won the grand prix rally.

Another daughter, Charlotte,
she was a filthy harlot,
her thighs at night were lily-white,
but in the morning scarlet.

The ship's dog's name was Rover,
the whole crew did him over;
they ground and ground that poor old hound
from Land's End round to Dover.

The ship's cat's name was Kitty;
her arse was black and shitty;
her feline twat was kept red-hot
by a crew who knew no pity.

The crew were different races,
you could see it in their faces;
they were always frigging against the rigging
for want of better places.

Their leader's name was Paul,
he only had one ball,
but with that cracker he rolled tobacco
around the wheelhouse wall.

When in the Adriatic
the crew were quite ecstatic;
the rise and fall of cock and ball
was almost automatic.

The captain was elated,
the crew investigated;
they found some sand in his prostate gland –
he had to be castrated.

So now we end this serial
from sheer lack of material;
I wish you luck, whenever you fuck,
from all disease venereal.

CATS ON THE ROOFTOPS

To the tune of "John Peel".

Cats on the rooftops, cats on the tiles,
cats with syphilis and cats with piles,
cats with their arseholes wreathed in smiles,
as they revel in the joys of copulation.

The donkey on the common is a solitary moke,
and it's very very seldom that he gets a poke,
but when he does, he lets it soak,
as he revels in the joys of copulation.

The baboon's arse is red and white,
there's a glow below like a neon light,
and it waves like a flag in the jungle night,
as he revels in the joys of copulation.

The hippopotamus, or so it seems,
very rarely has wet dreams,
but when he does, he comes in streams,
as he revels in the joys of copulation.

In Egypt now, the crocodile
only has a naughty once in a while,
but when he does, he floods the Nile,
as he revels in the joys of copulation.

The old rhinoceros is just like us,
he'll have a naughty without any fuss,

and when he comes, he comes like pus,
as he revels in the joys of copulation.

The elephant's rump is thick and round,
a small one weighs a thousand pound;
two together shake the ground,
as they revel in the joys of copulation.

The poor gorilla, or so it appears,
never gets a grind in a thousand years,
but when he does, he makes up for arrears,
as he revels in the joys of copulation.

The old dromedary's a screaming fairy,
his tool is bent and his balls are hairy,
and when he comes, it's something scary,
as he revels in the joys of copulation.

The old wild boar, in the mud all day,
thinks of the sows that are far, far away,
and the corkscrew motion that lasts half a day,
as he revels in the joys of copulation.

The camel likes to have his fun,
his night's complete when he gets done;
he always gets two humps for one,
as he revels in the joys of copulation.

But the poor desert camel has no water for a week,
and as he doesn't drink, the poor old bugger
    cannot leak,
so he has to hold his water, so to speak,
as he revels in the joys of copulation.

The ape is small and rather slow;
erect he stands a foot or so,
so when he comes, it's time to go,
as he revels in the joys of copulation.

The ostrich in the desert is a solitary chick,
without the opportunity to dip his wick,
but when he does, it slips in quick,
as he revels in the joys of copulation.

The whale is a mammal, as everybody knows;
he takes two days to do it, but when he's in the
        throes,
he doesn't stop to take it out, but piddles through
        his nose,
as he revels in the joys of copulation.

Sheep in the sheepfold, sheep in lamb,
sheep in agony, sheep in a jam,
sheep being done by a bloody great ram,
as they revel in the joys of copulation.

Bulls in the paddock, bulls in the corn,
bulls with balls and bulls with a horn,
bulls with their cocks all shaven and shorn,
as they revel in the joys of copulation.

The old kangaroo, how he loves a do;
he'll have a naughty with any old roo,
and when he comes, he comes like glue,
as he revels in the joys of copulation.

The Australian lady emu, when she wants to find
     a mate,
wanders round the desert with a feather up her
     date.
You should see that feather quiver when she
     meets her destined fate,
as she revels in the joys of copulation.

The poor domestic doggie, on the chain all day,
never gets a chance to let himself go gay,
so he licks at his dick in a frantic way,
as he revels in the joys of copulation.

The dainty little skylark sings a very pretty song,
he has a ponderous penis fully forty cubits long;
you should hear his high crescendo when his mate
     is on the prong,
as he revels in the joys of copulation.

The owls in the trees, and the cats on the tiles,
one screws in solitude, the other in files;
you can hear the howls and shrieks for miles,
as they revel in the joys of copulation.

Old brother tortoise lives in his shell,
he can't get at it very well,
but when he does, cor bloody hell!
as he revels in the joys of copulation.

Frogs on the seashore, frogs on the rocks,
frogs with the clap and frogs with the pox,

frogs with warts and festering cocks
as they revel in the joys of copulation.

The dirty little bedbug has his morals torn to bits
when he sees a husband playing with his wife's
        rosy tits,
so he reaches out and fornicates a thousand million
        nits
as he revels in the joys of copulation.

The queen bees flit among the trees,
and there consort with whom they please;
they fill the land with sons of bees,
as they revel in the joys of copulation.

The oyster is a model of chastity,
and you can't tell the he from the she,
but she can tell, and so can he,
as they revel in the joys of copulation.

Long-legged curates grind like goats,
pale-faced spinsters screw like stoats,
and the whole damn world stands by and gloats,
as they revel in the joys of copulation.

The lady by the seashore was feeling rather
        blue;
she saw the others at it, and she thought it
        wouldn't do,
so she bought three bananas, and she ate the other
        two,
as she revelled in the joys of copulation.

The labours of the poofter find but little favour here,
but the morally leprous bastard has a peaceful
    sleep, I fear,
as he dreams he rips a red 'un up some dirty
    bugger's rear,
as he revels in the joys of copulation.

The poor old creeping Jesus, of his morals there's
    no doubt;
he walks around St Kilda with his doodle hanging
    out,
and when he sees a wench it up and hits him in
    the snout,
as he revels in the thought of copulation.

The regimental sergeant major leads a miserable
    life,
he can't afford a mistress and he doesn't have a
    wife,
so he rams it up the bottom of the regimental fife,
as he revels in the joys of copulation.

You wake up in the morning with a roaring stand
and a peculiar feeling in your seminary gland,
and there's no one home so you take yourself in
    hand,
and revel in the joys of masturbation.

Thirty-four verses, all in rhyme,
to sit and sing them seems a crime,
when we could better spend our time,
revelling in the joys of copulation!

O'REILLY'S DAUGHTER

To the tune of "The One-eyed Reilly".

Sitting in O'Reilly's bar
I was a-drinking gin and water;
suddenly it came to mind:
like to shag O'Reilly's daughter.

    Titty-i-i, titty-i-i,
    titty-i-i the one-eyed Reilly,
    jig-a-jig jig, frig a little pig,
    jig-a-jig jig très bon.

Her hair was black, her eyes were blue,
the colonel, major and captain sought her,
the company goat and the drummer too,
but they never got into O'Reilly's daughter.

O Jack O'Sullivan is my name,
I'm the king of copulation,
drinking gin my claim to fame,
shagging girls my occupation.

Well, walking through the park that day
who should I meet but O'Reilly's daughter;
never a word I had to say
but, 'Don't you think we really oughter?'

Up the stairs and into bed,
I gently cocked my left leg over;

never a word the maiden said,
laughed like hell till the fun was over.

I banged her till her tits were flat,
filled her up with soapy water
enough to make a dozen brats –
if she doesn't have twins she really oughter.

Heard some footsteps on the stair,
who should it be but her bloody old father?
Two horse-pistols in his belt,
looking for the man who'd had his daughter.

Grabbed O'Reilly by the hair,
shoved his face in a bucket of water,
rammed the pistols up his butt
a damn sight harder than I shagged his daughter.

Now O'Reilly's dead and gone,
now O'Reilly is no more;
we've got hold of his coffin lid,
going to use it for a door.

Now come ye lasses, come ye maids,
answer now and don't speak shyly:
would yez have it straight and true,
or the way I give it to the one-eyed Reilly?

Titty-i-i, titty-i-i,
titty-i-i the one-eyed Reilly,
rub-a-dub dub, balls and all,
play it on your old base drum.

THE HARLOT
OF JERUSALEM

To the tune of "Kafoozalum".

Down in the land of King Farouk
there lived a girl of ill-repute,
a prostitute, a bloody beaut,
the harlot of Jerusalem.

> *Hi ho Kafoozalum,*
> *Kafoozalum, Kafoozalum,*
> *Hi ho Kafoozalum,*
> *the harlot of Jerusalem.*

Kafoozalum was a wily witch,
a warty whore, a brazen bitch,
who caused all the pricks to itch,
right throughout Jerusalem.

The floors, the halls, the Wailing Wall,
were all festooned with the balls
and tools of fools who tried to ride
the harlot of Jerusalem.

And though she'd whored for many a year,
of pregnancy she had no fear;
she washed her passage out with beer,
the best in all Jerusalem.

A student lived beneath the wall,
and though he'd only got one ball,
he'd been through all, or nearly all
the harlots of Jerusalem.

His phallic limb was lean and tall,
his sex technique caused all to fall;
his victims lined the Wailing Wall
that runs around Jerusalem.

One night returning from a spree,
although he didn't have the fee,
he decided then and there to see
the harlot of Jerusalem.

He walked in through the brothel door
and laid her on the earthen floor,
to have his fill of that old whore
the harlot of Jerusalem.

He took her to a shady nook
and from his pants he gently took
a penis like a butcher's hook,
the pride of all Jerusalem.

He whopped it up between her thighs,
it damn near reached up to her eyes,
but all she gave was a couple of sighs,
the harlot of Jerusalem.

He laid her down upon her bum,
and, shooting like an Owen gun,
he sowed the seed of many a son
within the fair Kafoozalum.

It was a sight to make you sick
to hear him grunt so fast and quick
while rending with his crooked prick
the womb of fair Kafoozalum.

But then there came an Israelite,
a lusty, boasting, bragging skite,
who'd vowed that he would spend that night
with the harlot of Jerusalem.

It was for her no fortune good
that he should want to flash his pud;
he mostly hung about the wood
and perved on all Jerusalem.

He loathed the art of copulation,
for his delight was masturbation,
for which he'd pay with great elation
the whores of old Jerusalem.

And though he paid his women well,
this syphilitic spawn of hell,
somehow each year they tolled the bell
for ten whores of Jerusalem.

So when he saw the grunting pair,
with roars of rage he rent the air,
and vowed that he would soon take care
of the harlot of Jerusalem.

Upon the earth he found a stick
to which he fastened half a brick
and took a swipe at the mighty prick
of the student of Jerusalem.

He gave the pair a dirty look
and grabbed the student by his crook
and tossed him into Kedron's brook
that flows hard by Jerusalem.

The student gave a mighty roar
and swore he'd even up the score;
in the harlot's arse a hole he bore
that even stretched Kafoozalum.

He stepped back full of rage and fight
and grabbed that perving Israelite,
and rammed him up with all his might
the arsehole of Kafoozalum.

The wily whore she knew her part;
she gave a squeeze and blew a fart
that sent him flying like a dart
right across Jerusalem.

Across the sea of Galilee
he was buzzing like a bumblebee,
till he caught his balls upon a tree
that grows in old Jerusalem.

And to this day you still can see
his balls a-hanging in that tree;
let that to you a warning be
when passing through Jerusalem.

And when the moon is bright and red
a eunuch ghost flies overhead,
still raining curses on the bed
of that brazen bitch Kafoozalum.

As for the student and his lass,
many a playful night did pass
until she joined the VD class
for harlots in Jerusalem.

And even then the randy slut
would leave the town and work her butt
beside the Salvation Army hut
in the old part of Jerusalem.

This harlot lived for many a year
till sterilised by gonorrhoea,
and men of taste would not go near
the harlot of Jerusalem.

But all you other randy folk
who love to have your nightly poke
can still pay the fee and let it soak
in the harlot of Jerusalem.

THE OLD LADIES LOCKED IN THE LAVATORY

To the tune of "Oh Dear, What Can the Matter Be".

O dear, what can the matter be?
Twenty-one old ladies locked in the lavatory;
they were there from Sunday to Saturday,
nobody knew they were there.

They said they were off to have tea with the vicar,
they went in together, they thought it was quicker,
but the lavatory door was a bit of a sticker,
and the vicar had tea all alone.

The first was the wife of a deacon in Dover
and though she was known as a bit of a rover
she liked it so much she thought she'd stay over
and nobody knew she was there.

The second one's name was Elizabeth Draper
went in with the hope that someone might rape her
but all that she got was some pink toilet paper
and nobody knew she was there.

The third was an athletic lady named Myrtle
who hopped over the door like a steeplechase
    hurdle

and suspended herself from the stay in her girdle
and nobody knew she was there.

The fourth one's name was Josephine Fryer;
she kept on forever, she couldn't retire;
the level of water rose higher and higher
and nobody knew she was there.

The fifth was the Bishop of Chichester's daughter
who went in to pass some superfluous water;
she pulled on the chain, and the rising tide caught
    her
and nobody knew she was there.

The sixth old lady was old Mrs Brickle
who found herself caught in a desperate pickle –
stuck in a paybooth without even a nickel,
and nobody knew she was there.

The seventh old lady was Abigail Humphrey
who settled inside to make herself comfy
but then she found out she could not get her bum
    free
and nobody knew she was there.

The eighth old lady was Ermyntrude Bender
who only went in to adjust her suspender
but the end got caught up in her feminine gender
and nobody knew she was there.

The ninth was a lady named Jennifer Trim
who only sat down on a personal whim

but she somehow got caught 'twixt the cup and
    the brim
and nobody knew she was there.

The tenth old lady was Caroline Carter
who had some renown as a soloist farter;
she sat down and puffed out 'The Moonlight
    Sonata'
and nobody knew she was there.

The eleventh old lady was Madeline Proctor
and she was the wife of a Harley Street doctor;
it was the things he flushed down the toilet that
    shocked her
and nobody knew she was there.

The twelfth old lady was old Mrs Bligh
who went in with a bottle to booze on the sly;
she stood on the seat and fell in with a cry,
and nobody knew she was there.

The thirteenth one was Mary-Lou Porter
who had a constriction when passing her water
but she managed to dribble a pint and a quarter
and nobody knew she was there.

The fourteenth lady was Gabrielle Jepson;
she had just taken a large dose of Epsom,
and o! the result! It was flotsam and jetsam,
and nobody knew she was there.

The fifteenth one was Melanie Ruffin;
she tried for an hour but couldn't do nuffin.

She said, 'That was good!' but they knew she was
    bluffin'
and nobody knew she was there.

The sixteenth's name was Lorelei Mason;
she swallowed a seed which commenced
    germination,
and there she took root in a queer situation
and nobody knew she was there.

The seventeenth was Gwendolyn Tanner
who'd swallowed a flute on a trip to Havana;
she farted – and out came 'The Star Spangled
    Banner'
and nobody knew she was there.

The eighteenth lady was Jacqueline Muddle
who dropped off to sleep at the height of her
    huddle;
she woke with a start with her bum in a puddle
and nobody knew she was there.

The nineteenth one was Sue Ellen Hooper
who said, 'Why, these fittings are quite
    super-duper;
the paper, I find, makes a fine pooper-scooper',
and nobody knew she was there.

The twentieth old lady was Sophia Mollish;
four bits of paper she found she'd demolish:
one down wipe, one up wipe, one dry wipe, one
    polish,
and nobody knew she was there.

The last old lady was Hildegard Schreiner
who thought that wanking was a city in China
until she found Smirnoff – and now they can't
    find her
and nobody knew she was there.

O dear, what a calamity!
Lots of old ladies locked in the lavatory,
they were there from Sunday to Saturday,
and nobody knew they were there.

THE GAY CABALLERO

To the tune of "The Spanish Nobilio".

There once was a gay caballero,
an extremely gay caballero,
and of course he had a roto-maree,
a beautiful roto-maree-o.

He went to a low-down casino,
an extremely low-down casino,
and of course he took his roto-maree,
his roto-, roto-maree-o.

He met a fair senorita,
an extremely fair senorita,
and of course he inserted his roto-maree,
his roto-, roto-maree-o.

He caught a filthy disease-o,
an extremely filthy disease-o,
slap-bang on the tip of his roto-maree,
his roto-, roto-maree-o.

He went to a learned doctrano,
an extremely learned doctrano,
who snipped off the tip of his roto-maree,
his roto-, roto-maree-o.

Now he sits by a swift-flowing rio,
an extremely swift-flowing rio,

lamenting the loss of his roto-maree,
his beautiful roto-maree-o.

Now listen you filthy backstreeters,
if you want to go lay senoritas,
and you don't want the pox,
shove socks on the tops
of your roto-, roto-maree-os.

THE WOODPECKER'S SONG

To the tune of "Dixie".

I put my finger in the woodpecker's hole,
the woodpecker said 'God bless my soul!
Pull it out! Pull it out! Pull it out!
Re-move it!'

I took my finger from the woodpecker's hole,
the woodpecker said 'God bless my soul!
Put it back! Put it back! Put it back!
Re-place it!'

I stuck my finger in the woodpecker's hole,
the woodpecker said 'God bless my soul!
Turn it round! Turn it round! Turn it round!
Re-volve it!'

I turned my finger in the woodpecker's hole,
the woodpecker said 'God bless my soul!
Turn it back! Turn it back! Turn it back!
Re-verse it!'

I rotated my finger in the woodpecker's hole,
the woodpecker said 'God bless my soul!
Back and forth! Back and forth! Back and forth!
Re-ciprocate it!'

I plunged my finger in the woodpecker's hole,
the woodpecker said 'God bless my soul!
Take it out! Take it out! Take it out!
Re-tract it!'

I withdrew my finger from the woodpecker's hole,
the woodpecker said 'God bless my soul!
Have a whiff! Have a whiff! Have a whiff!
Re-volting!'

SHE WAS POOR BUT SHE WAS HONEST

To its own traditional tune.

She was poor, but she was honest,
victim of the squire's whim;
first he loved her, then he left her,
and she had a child by him.

> *It's the same the whole world over,*
> *it's the poor what gets the blame,*
> *it's the rich has all the pleasure,*
> *ain't it all a bloody shame!*

See him with his hounds and horses,
drinking champagne in his club,
while the victim of his passions
swills her Guinness in a pub.

So she went away to London
for to hide her grief and pain;
there she met an army chaplain
and she lost her name again.

See him as he jaws the soldiers,
preaching of the flames of hell,
while she treads the pavements, selling
the only thing she has to sell.

See her on the bridge at midnight
throwing kisses at the moon;
she says 'Jack, I've never 'ad it' –
but she spoke too bloody soon.

See her hanging round in Soho
picking blackheads from her crutch;
she says, 'George, I've never done it';
says he, 'Not bloody much!'

So she walked the streets of London
sinking deeper in her shame
till she met a Labour leader
and again she lost her name.

See him in the House of Commons
making laws to put down crime
while the victim of his passions
walks the streets in mud and slime.

See him riding in a carriage
past the gutter where she stands;
he has made a stylish marriage
while she wrings her ringless hands.

See him sitting in the theatre
in the front row with the best
while the girl that he has ruined
entertains a sordid guest.

See her now in the theatre
sitting in the front-row stalls,

in the frenzy of her passion
grabbing strange men by the balls.

See him sitting in the pictures
throwing peanuts in the pit
while the girl that he has ruined
tramps her way through mud and shit.

See him at his country mansion
riding gaily to the hunt
while the victim of his folly
earns her living selling flowers.

See her down in Piccadilly
selling matches, penny a box,
while the men that she has been with
carry round their load of pox.

See her stand in Piccadilly
offering up her aching quim
which is now completely ruined,
and it's all because of him.

Then there came a lordly bishop,
marriage was the tale he told;
there was no one else to take her,
so she sold her soul for gold.

See her in her horse and carriage
driving idly through the park;
though she made a wealthy marriage,
still she hides a broken heart.

In a cottage down in Sussex
see her parents old and lame
drink the champagne what she sends them,
but they never speak her name.

See him riding in his Bentley
coming homewards from the hunt;
he got riches from his marriage,
she's got corns upon her feet.

See her standing at the wash-tub
washing out his gartered socks
while he's busy in the vestry
feeling up the choir-boys' cocks.

So she left his ancestral mansions
and those tall and stately halls
and as she walks the streets of London
damns and blasts his bloody balls.

See him in the church on Sunday
preaching sermons upon crime
while the girl that he abandoned
is selling chunks of her behind.

She's got corns and horrid chancres
in the plumbing of her guts
so she leapt into the river
for to give her poor life up.

See her on that bridge at midnight
saying, 'Farewell, blighted love.'

Then a scream, a splash – oh goodness,
what is she a-doing of?

Then they dragged her from the river,
water from her clothes they wrang,
and they thought that she had had it,
when the corpse got up and sang,

*'It's the same the whole world over,
it's the poor what gets the blame,
it's the rich takes all the gravy,
ain't it all a bleeding shame!'*

JOHN BROWN'S PENIS

To the tune of "John Brown's Body".

John Brown's penis was a bloody horrible sight,
covered up with syphilis and little bits of shite,
but the funny thing about it was it seemed to work
    all right,
now he's gone to a far better land.

    O, the hoary old seducer,
    O, the hoary old seducer,
    O, the hoary old seducer,
    but he still keeps rogering on.

John Brown's penis was of inches quite eleven;
he began to masturbate when he was only seven;
the feeling that he got was his initial taste of
    heaven,
and he still keeps rogering on.

Now he's gone to a land of everlasting bliss,
where there ain't no gono and there ain't no
    syphilis,
constrictions of the arsehole and constrictions
    when you piss,
he's gone to a far better land.

John Brown's standing on the Hallelujah shore,
gonorrhoea and syphilis will trouble him no more,

for now he's got the Holy Virgin Mary for a whore
as he still keeps rogering on.

Among the pretty angels he is making all the
        rounds,
and now the Virgin Mary has put him out of
        bounds
for claiming to be the Trinity on insufficient
        grounds
as he still goes rogering on.

IF I WERE THE MARRYING KIND, SIR

To the tune of "One Man Went to Mow".

If I were the marrying kind, sir,
which, thank the Lord, I'm not, sir,
the girl I'd wed to share my bed
would be a fullback's daughter.

For she'd kick hard, and I'd kick hard,
and we'd kick hard together,
and we'd be right in the middle of the night
kicking hard together.

and so on through the other positions:
centre three-quarter's daughter: she'd break
     through . . .
winger's daughter: she'd run hard . . .
prop's daughter: she'd bind tight . . .
lock's daughter: she'd lock hard . . .
fly-half's daughter: she'd whip it out . . .
scrum-half's daughter: she'd put it in . . .
five-eighth's daughter: she'd pass it out . . .
hooker's daughter: she'd strike hard . . .
second-row's daughter: she'd push hard . . .
ballboy's daughter: she'd hold balls . . .
referee's daughter: she'd blow hard . . .
Rugby fan's daughter: she'd root hard . . .

LIFE PRESENTS A DISMAL PICTURE

To the tune of "Deutschland über Alles".

Life presents a dismal picture,
black and dark as any tomb;
father has an anal stricture,
mother has a fallen womb.
Sister Sue has been aborted
for the sixty-second time;
Uncle Joe has been deported
for a homosexual crime.

Ours is not a happy household;
no one ever laughs or smiles.
Mine's a dismal occupation,
cracking ice for Grandpa's piles.
Uncle Charlie has a chancre
caught from Uncle Henry's wife;
Maggie got her ovaries busted,
Auntie's at the change of life.

Brother Bill's emasculated
for the safety of the race;
sister Jean is now frustrated,
no man's safe around the place.
Jane the under-housemaid vomits
every morning just on eight,
to the horror of the butler,
who's the author of her fate.

Auntie Kate has diarrhoea,
shits ten times more than she ought,
stands all day at the rear,
lest she should be taken short.
And the kid is just another,
always having bloody fits;
every time it coughs it vomits,
every time it farts it shits.

Mabel's husband's now in prison
for a childish prank of mine;
pinching things that wasn't his 'n –
women's scanties off a line.
Little Jim keeps masturbating,
though we tell him it's a sin;
Uncle Peter's the Yorkshire Ripper,
Uncle Henry dobbed him in.

Dad's a man who likes the bestial,
incest is my mother's fun,
so the whole four sleep together –
father, mother, horse, and son.
Anal-oral trends disgust me,
though pronounced in Tiny Tim;
I prefer a sixty-niner –
he sucks me and I suck him.

Father he has lost his manhood,
mother she has got the whites;
someone must be diddling Mabel,
for she don't come home of nights.
Nannie she has got a baby,
and we don't know who's its dad;
Johnny has a case of syphilis –
and by damn he's got it bad.

Little Jimmy's in the nuthouse,
looks like he'll be there for good.
And the cause of his misfortune?
Too much pulling of his pud.
Yet we are not disappointed,
neither are we up the spout;
Auntie Mabel has just farted,
blown her arsehole inside out.

RAILWAY BLUES

To the tune of "Humoresque".

Passengers will please refrain
from using toilet while the train
is standing at the station or at rest;
tramps and hobos underneath
might get it in their hair and teeth,
which really isn't what they like the best.

If you wish to pass some water
kindly call the guard or porter
who'll place a vessel in the vestibule;
we believe in constipation
while the train is at the station –
thank you for observance of this rule!

Pissing while the train is moving
is another way of proving
that control of eye and hand is sure;
we like our passengers to be neat
so please don't piss upon the seat –
or even worse, don't piss upon the floor.

If the ladies' room is taken,
never feel the least forsaken,
never show a sign of sad defeat;
try the gents across the hall,
and if some man has had the call,
he'll courteously relinquish you his seat.

If these efforts are in vain
then simply break the window pane
(this novel method's used by very few);
we go strolling through the park
goosing statues in the dark –
if Peter Pan can take it, why can't you?

ARSEHOLE-CHARCOAL

To the tune of "The Vicar of Bray".

Two tom cats by the fireside sat
all round a bucket of charcoal.
Said one tom cat to the other tom cat,
'Let's blacken each other's arsehole.'
Arsehole, charcoal, charcoal, arsehole,
all round a bucket of charcoal,
so one took a piece and the other took a piece
and they blackened each other's arsehole.

Three tom cats by the fireside sat ... *etc.*

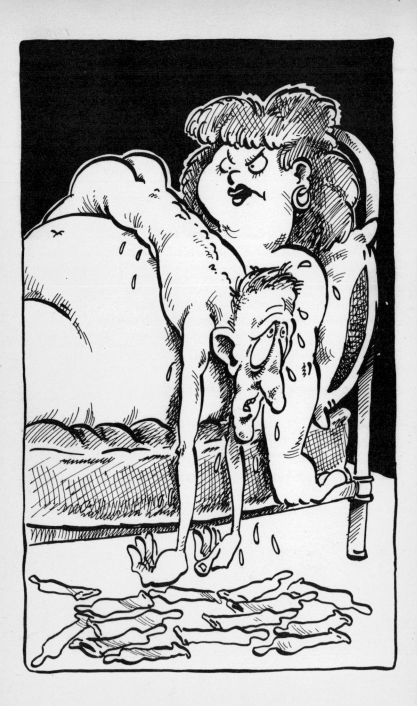

ON TOP OF OLD SOPHIE

To the tune of "On Top of Old Smokey".

On top of old Sophie, all covered in sweat,
I've used fourteen rubbers, and she hasn't come
    yet.

For screwing's a pleasure, and farting's relief,
but a long-winded lover brings nothing but grief.

She'll kiss you and hug you, say it won't take too
        long.
but two hours later you're still going strong.

So come all you lovers and listen to me:
don't waste your erection on a long-winded she.

For your root will just wither, and your passion
        will die,
and she will forsake you, and you'll never know
        why.

ESKIMO NELL

Recitation.

When a man grows old and his balls grow cold,
and the tip of his knob turns blue,
looking back on a life of struggle and strife,
he can tell you a tale or two.
So fill my glass and I'll park my arse
and a tale to you I'll tell
of Deadeye Dick and his muscular prick,
and a whore named Eskimo Nell.

Now Deadeye Dick and Mexico Pete
had been working Dead Man's Creek,
and they'd had no luck in the way of a fuck
for nigh on half a week,
just a moose or two, and a caribou,
and a bison-cow or so;
since Deadeye Dick's was the king of pricks
he found this fucking slow.

So Deadeye Dick and Mexico Pete
set out in search of fun,
with Deadeye Dick wielding the prick,
and Mexico Pete the gun.
And when Deadeye Dick and Mexico Pete
are sore, depressed, and sad,
it's mainly cunt that bears the brunt,
so the shooting ain't too bad.

So do or dare this horny pair
set out for the Rio Grande,
Deadeye Dick with his mighty prick,
and Pete with his gun in his hand.
And as they blazed their randy trail
no man their path withstood,
and many a bride, her husband's pride,
knew pregnant widowhood.

They made the strand of the Rio Grande
at the height of a blazing noon,
and to slake their thirst and do their worst
they sought Red Mike's saloon,
came crashing in with doors aswing,
both prick and gun flashed free:
'According to sex, you poxy wrecks,
you drinks or fucks with me.'

Now they knew the fame of our hero's name
from the Horn to Panama,
so with nothing worse than a muttered curse
those dagos sought the bar.
And the women too his habits knew,
down there on the Rio Grande,
so forty whores whipped down their drawers
at Deadeye Dick's command.

They saw the fingers of Mexico Pete
twitch on the pistol grip;
at a fearful rate – for they dared not wait –
those whores began to strip.
Now Deadeye Dick was breathing quick,
with lecherous snorts and grunts,
as forty arses were bared to view,
to say nothing of forty cunts.

Now forty arses and forty cunts,
you'll see if you use your wits,
and are pretty slick at arithmetic,
make all of eighty tits.
And fourscore tits are a gladsome sight
to a man with a mighty stand;
they may be rare in Berkeley Square,
but not on the Rio Grande.

Now Deadeye Dick had screwed a few
on a spree the previous night;
this he had done in a spirit of fun,
to whet his appetite.
His phallic limb was in fucking trim
as he backed and took a run;
he took a jump at the nearest rump
and scored a hole in one.

He bore that whore to the sandy floor
and fairly fucked her fine,
and though she grinned, it put the wind
up the other thirty-nine.
When Deadeye Dick performs this trick
he's got no time to spare;
with speed and length combined with strength
he fairly singes hair.

Now Deadeye Dick he fucks 'em quick;
he cast the first aside,
and made a dart at the second tart
– when the swing doors opened wide.
Then there entered in to that hall of sin,
into that harlot's hell,
a lusty maid who was unafraid;
her name was Eskimo Nell.

Now Deadeye Dick had got his prick
well into number two
when Eskimo Nell let out a yell
and hollered, 'Hey there, you!'
Dick sprang about with an angry shout;
his face and knob were red;
with a dextrous flick of his muscular prick
the whore flew over his head.

Nell glanced our hero up and down,
and looked him in the eye;
with utter scorn she scanned the horn
that rose from his hairy thigh.
She stubbed out the butt of her cigarette
on the end of his steaming knob,
and so utterly beat was Mexico Pete
that he failed to do his job.

It was Eskimo Nell who broke the spell
in accents calm and cool:
'You cunt-struck simp of a Yankee pimp,
you call that thing a tool?
If this here town can't take that down,'
she sneered to the cowering whores,
'there's one little cunt can do the stunt,
but it's Eskimo Nell's – not yours.'

She shed her garments one by one
with an air of conscious pride
till at last she stood in her womanhood,
and they saw the Great Divide.
It's fair to state it was not so great,
but it had a solid rim;
viewed from without it left no doubt
of the tensile strength within.

She spread herself on a table-top
where someone had left a glass;
with a twitch of her tits she crushed it to bits
between the cheeks of her arse.
She flexed her knees with supple ease
and spread her legs apart;
with an offhand nod to the randy sod
she gave him the cue to start.

But Dick also knew a trick or two,
and meant to take his time;
a miss like this was coital bliss,
so he played a pantomime.
He flicked his foreskin up and down,
and made his balls inflate
till they looked like a couple of granite knobs
on top of a garden gate.

He winked his arsehole in and out
as his balls increased in size;
his mighty prick grew twice as thick
till it almost reached his eyes.
He smothered his rod with rum and gob
to make it piping hot,
and to finish the job he peppered the knob
with a cayenne pepper-pot.

He didn't back to take a run,
or make a flying leap;
he didn't swoop; he began to stoop
in a steady forward creep.
Then he took a sight as a gunman might
along that fearsome tool,
and the dead slow glide as it slid inside
was calculating, cool.

Now you've seen the pistons working
on the mighty CPR
with the driving force of a thousand horse –
well, you know what pistons are;
or you think you do, if you've yet to view
the power that drives that prick,
or the work that's done on a non-stop run
by a man like Deadeye Dick.

But Eskimo Nell was an infidel,
and as good as a whole harem,
with the strength of ten in her abdomen
and her Rock of Ages beam.
Amidships she could stand a rush
like the flush of a water-closet,
and she gripped Dick's cock like the Chatswood
        lock
on the National Safe Deposit.

Now Deadeye Dick would not come
        quick;
he meant to reserve his powers.
When he'd a mind he'd grind and grind
for a couple of solid hours.
So Nell lay for a while with a subtle smile,
then her vice-like grip grew keener;
with a languid sigh she sucked him dry
with the ease of a vacuum cleaner.

She performed this feat in a way so neat
as to set at complete defiance
the basic laws that govern the course
of normal sexual science.
She calmly rode through the phallic code
that for years had stood the test,

and accepted rules of the established schools
in a second or two went west!

And so my friend we approach the end
of this copulative epic;
the effect on Dick was sudden and quick
and akin to anaesthetic.
He slid to the floor and knew no more,
his passion extinct and dead;
he didn't shout as his tool came out,
though it must have stripped the thread.

Then Mexico Pete he sprang to his feet
to avenge his pal's affront;
his long-nosed Colt, with a jarring jolt,
he rammed right up her cunt.
He rammed it hard to trigger guard,
and fired it twice times three.
To his surprise she rolled her eyes
and squealed in ecstasy.

As she rose to her feet she looked so sweet;
'Bully,' she cried, 'for you!
Though I might have guessed it's about the best
you Yankee simps can do.
When next, my friend, you two intend
to sally forth for fun,
get Deadeye Dick a sugar-stick,
and buy yourself a bun.

'I'm going back to the frozen North,
where the pricks are hard and strong,
back to the land of the all-night stand –
and the nights are six months long!

Where you stick it in as hard as tin,
the land where spunk is spunk,
not a trickling stream of lukewarm cream,
but a solid frozen chunk.

'That's the land where they understand
what it is to copulate;
where even the dead share a common bed
and the babies masturbate.
And in that land of the grinding gland,
where the walrus plays with his prong,
where the polar bear wanks off in his lair,
that's where they'll sing this song.

'They'll tell this tale on the Arctic trail
where the nights are sixty below,
where it's so damn cold French letters are sold
wrapped up in a ball of snow.
In the Valley of Death, with baited breath,
that's where they'll sing it too;
where the skeletons rattle in sexual battle,
and the mouldering corpses screw.

'Yes, I'm going forth to the frozen North,
where a whore can do no wrong,
where the Arctic blizzard sticks deep in your
    gizzard,
like fourteen inches of dong;
back again to where men are men,
to the Terra Bollicum;
I go, my friends, to a worthy end,
for the North is calling *"Come!"'*

And Deadeye Dick and Mexico Pete
slunk out of the Rio Grande;
Deadeye Dick with a useless prick,
and Pete with no gun in his hand.
For when a man grows old and his balls grow cold
and the tip of his prick turns blue,
and the hole in the middle refuses to piddle –
I'd say he was fucked, wouldn't you?